Especially for

Amanda & Patrick

From

April

Date

Christmas
_2011_

"I believe in the sun even when it's not shining. I believe in love even when not feeling it. I believe in _God_ even when He is silent.."

— Anonymous

A CELEBRATION OF FAMILY

*A Keepsake Devotional Featuring the
Inspirational Verse of Helen Steiner Rice*

BARBOUR
PUBLISHING

CONTENTS

INTRODUCTION

When it comes to home and family, Helen Steiner Rice is in her element. Her verse is rich with inspiration, understanding, and insight into traditional family values. She boldly illuminates the role of father and aptly describes the tough and tender heart of mothers. She applauds the love that brings them together and the joy of family life that follows. She also reminds us that God must be the central figure in our homes if our families are to fulfill the purposes God intends.

We hope that you will be challenged by the devotionals that have been added to complement the poems. They have been woven together to celebrate the extraordinary nature of family.

No matter how wonderful, strange, unique, talented, loving, dysfunctional, amusing, or oddly embarrassing your family may be, theirs were the first faces you looked into and the first voices you heard. They have influenced you both for good and for bad. And they have taught you what makes a family strong and what tears a family apart. And now you have the privilege and the responsibility to work to make your family a place of love, instruction, kindness, and truth. Let Helen show you the way.

LOVE ONE ANOTHER AS
I HAVE LOVED YOU

"*L*ove one another as I have loved you"
May seem impossible to do,
But if you will try to trust and believe,
Great are the joys you will receive.
For love makes us patient,
understanding, and kind,
And we judge with our hearts and
not with our minds.
For as soon as love entered
the heart's open door,
The faults we once saw are
not there anymore.

And the things that seem wrong
begin to look right
When viewed in the softness of
love's gentle light.
For love works in ways that are
wondrous and strange,
And there is nothing in life that
love cannot change.
And all that God promised will
someday come true
When you love one another the
way He loved you.

~HSR

Celebrating the
Two of Us

Remember These Words

We are gathered together
   on this happy day
To stand before God and
   to reverently say,
"I take thee to be my
   partner for life,
To love and to live with as
   husband and wife,
To have and to hold forever,
   sweetheart,
Through sickness and health,
   until death do us part,
To love and to cherish
   whatever betide,
And in better or worse to
   stand by your side."

~HSR

HEAVENLY PROMISES

*"I have placed my rainbow in the clouds. It is a sign of
my covenant with you and with all the earth."*
GENESIS 9:13 NLT

*I*f you have ever seen a rainbow from the window of an airplane, you may have been surprised to find that it looked quite different from that vantage point than it would have looked if your feet had been planted firmly on the ground. From the ground a rainbow appears as an arch from land to land, but in the sky, the rainbow forms a circle, symbolizing God's eternal promise to humankind.

A wedding ring is a circle as well, symbolizing a promise between two people on the day they say, "I do!" When that wedding ring goes on your finger, you make a promise to stand side by side and weather every storm, though you have no way of knowing what you might encounter in the days and years ahead. All you know is that you have decided to face life's uncertainties together.

You may now be five decades, five years, or five days into your marriage journey. Or you may not have even begun. Whatever the case, married life is filled with challenges—the nitty-gritty of everyday life. That's the purpose of the wedding ring. Whether it is a simple band or a glittering array of diamonds, its circular nature, like the rainbow, represents a promise that transcends the obstacles and surprises along the way.

The promise of the rainbow is secure in God's hands. Let Him help you secure your wedding promise as well.

THE MIRACLE
OF MARRIAGE

Marriage is the union of two people in love,
And love is sheer magic, for it's woven of
Gossamer dreams, enchantingly real,
That people in love are privileged to feel.
But the exquisite ecstasy that captures the heart
Of two people in love is just a small part
Of the beauty and wonder and miracle of
That growth and fulfillment and evolvement of love,
For only long years of living together
And caring and sharing in all kinds of weather
Both pleasure and pain, the glad and the sad,
Teardrops and laughter, the good and the bad
Can add new dimensions and lift love above
The rapturous ecstasies of falling in love.

~HSR

LOVING THE GOD WAY

"This is my command: Love one another the way I loved you.
This is the very best way to love."
JOHN 15:13 MSG

*S*ome think of love in terms of sunny blue skies and lilting song lyrics, yet love in its noblest and most miraculous form is love that makes one human being capable of laying down his or her life for another. This is a high standard, but one Jesus set when He came to earth dressed in human flesh and gave Himself for us. The good news is that God knows what we are made of. He understands that we are simply unable to love in this way without His help.

Of course love comes easily on sunshiny days, when everything is going our way. We revel in each other. But when difficult times come, when we are beset by unpleasant circumstances and asked to set our needs and desires aside in favor of what the other person wants, our human commitment to love is sorely tried. That's when we need to call on God to help us love as we should.

Don't settle for anything less in your marriage than the God kind of love. Surrender to it every day. This does not mean you should become a doormat; it means keeping the best interests of that other person always before you. Doing the right thing. Loving beyond your comfort zone.

WHAT IS MARRIAGE?

*I*t is sharing and caring,
　　Giving and forgiving,
Loving and being loved,
　　Walking hand in hand,
Talking heart to heart,
　　Seeing through each other's eyes,
Laughing together,
　　Weeping together,
Praying together,
　　And always trusting and believing
And thanking God for each other.
　　For love that is shared is a beautiful thing—
It enriches the soul and makes the heart sing.

~HSR

HEART TO HEART

He has made everything beautiful in its time.
He has also set eternity in the hearts of men; yet they cannot
fathom what God has done from beginning to end.
ECCLESIASTES 3:11

*H*ave you ever shown a child how to cut a heart from construction paper to make a valentine card? If so, you folded the paper in half and carefully cut half a heart. Then you unfolded the paper, and to the child's delight, a whole heart appeared.

This is a simple illustration of what happens in marriage. You are folded together in love and commitment. Over time, God shapes and molds you from two people into one. Then slowly and purposefully like a beautiful flower opening, your marriage unfolds— and there it is! You have become one heart, one flesh, complete in purpose, each side a reflection of the other.

Marriage works best when we yield ourselves to God's artistic hands. The folding and cutting process can be uncomfortable, even painful, at times, but in the end God makes something beautiful of it all. He works in the disagreements, the trouble, and the pain. You won't see the result for some time. But if you stand strong and stay close, the result is remarkable. God crafts your hearts into one and adds His blessing.

Allow God to use the sharp moments of life to create a beautiful partnership from two mismatched parts by folding and shaping you into one.

WITH GOD AS YOUR PARTNER

It takes a groom, it takes a bride—
   Two people standing side by side.
It takes a ring and vows that say
   This is our happy wedding day.
But wedding vows are sanctified
   And loving hearts are unified
When standing with the bride and groom,
   Unseen by others in the room,
The Spirit of the Lord is there
   To bless this happy bridal pair.
For God is love, and married life
   Is richer for both man and wife
When God becomes a partner, too,
   In everything they plan and do.

~HSR

FOLDING HANDS—
HOLDING HANDS

I want the men everywhere to pray, lifting up their hands
in a holy manner, without anger and arguments.

1 TIMOTHY 2:8 NCV

How many times have you heard the gentle command: "Bow your heads and fold your hands; it's time to pray"? Empty hands pressed together with fingers pointing toward heaven are the symbol of prayer. Like kneeling, folding your hands demonstrates humility and submission to God.

Prayer is an important part of a thriving, healthy marriage. It establishes a precedent of freely sharing your innermost thoughts, feelings, and dreams with each other and with God. In fact, few activities lead so effectively to openness and enhanced communication than the sharing and bonding and increased trust that come from prayer.

Prayer at meals around the table builds a bond of faith, always turning to God, recognizing our dependence on Him. Prayers at bedtime and before parting in the morning establish a pattern of trusting God and honoring Him not only as individuals but also as a family.

We live in a busy world with harried hearts and frantic schedules. Time will be an issue if you allow it to be. Even if you pray no more than a few words in the morning when you awaken or before you eat your breakfast, maybe even as you are saying good-bye for the day, it is worth the effort. God is eager to bless any effort you make.

WHEN TWO PEOPLE MARRY

Love that lasts forever must
  Be made of something strong—
The kind of strength that's gathered when
  The heart can hear no song.
When the sunshine of your wedding day
  Runs into stormy weather,
And hand in hand you brave the gale
  And climb steep hills together,
And clinging to each other
  While the thunder rolls above,
You seek divine protection
  In faith and hope and love.
For days of wine and roses
  Never make love's dreams come true—
It takes sacrifice and teardrops
  And problems shared by two
To give true love its beauty,
  Its grandeur and its fineness,
And to mold an earthly ecstasy
  Into heavenly divineness.

~HSR

ENDURING LOVE

[Love] bears all things, believes all things, hopes all things, endures all things.
1 CORINTHIANS 13:7 NKJV

As a child, you may have looked forward to your wedding day—a day you would never forget, ushering in a life of love and contentment. In the months and weeks before the big day, every detail was scrutinized and meticulously planned and rehearsed. Just like your love for each other, your big day and the life that followed would be picture perfect.

Is that how it actually happened?

More than likely, there were many small gaffes and imperfections. Perhaps your soloist flubbed a line or the musicians played the songs out of order. Did one of the bridesmaids trip on her dress? Maybe you put the ring on the wrong finger or stumbled over the words when you said your vows.

No matter how well you plan, such things happen. But those imperfections had no real effect at all on the business at hand. Your love for each other was strong and intense and towered over the details of the ceremony itself—so much so that over the years those "mistakes" became a delightful part of your common story.

Married life may have thrown you some curves as well—inconveniences, traumas, perhaps even tragedies. In those times, love has covered and supported you. It has strengthened and sustained you. In years to come, the love and faith you demonstrate in difficult times will beautify and enrich your lives together.

With Faith in Each Other and Faith in the Lord

With faith in each other
And faith in the Lord
May your marriage be blessed
With love's priceless reward,
For love that endures
And makes life worth living
Is built on strong faith
And unselfish giving.
So have faith, and the Lord
Will guide both of you through
The glorious new life
That is waiting for you.

~HSR

SEEDS OF FAITH

In him and through faith in him we may approach
God with freedom and confidence.
EPHESIANS 3:12

*H*ave you ever planted flower seeds, pressed them in, patted down the soil, watered them, and then waited for them to sprout? If you were a new gardener, you might even have caught yourself checking way too soon to see if the seeds were breaking through.

A practiced, patient gardener would know that there is simply nothing you can do to hurry the process along. Those seeds sprout when they are good and ready. In accordance with some deep inner code, they burst from their tiny dormant selves and push up through the earth in search of the light. So by faith you prepare the soil, plant the seeds, water the ground, and wait for the tiny shoots to appear. As you carefully tend the seedlings by supplying the water and sunlight they need, you will at some point be rewarded with bright, sweet-smelling blossoms.

The establishment of a good marriage is not something that happens during the hour of a wedding ceremony or even during months of engagement and wedding planning. It happens through faith—through trusting both your spouse and God when you can't see what is ahead.

With God's help and your tender care, your seeds of love will push upward toward the light of God's presence and your marriage will bloom and prosper.

For the New Bride

Now you're Mrs. instead of Miss,
    And you've sealed your wedding vows with a kiss.
Your future lies in your hands, my dear,
    For it's yours to mold from year to year.
God grant that you make it a beautiful thing,
    With all of the blessings that marriage can bring.
May you and that fine, lucky man of your choice
    Find daily new blessings to make you rejoice,
And year after year may you grow on together
    Always finding a rainbow regardless of weather. . .
And when youthful charms have faded away,
    May you look back with joy on your glad
    wedding day
And thank God for helping make you a wife
    Who discovered the blessings of a full married life.

~HSR

APRON KIND OF LOVE

"Whoever wants to become great among you must be your servant, and whoever wants to be first must be your slave—just as the Son of Man did not come to be served, but to serve, and to give his life as a ransom for many."
MATTHEW 20:26–28

Aprons, when they are used at all these days, are most often simple washable items. Sometimes they contain humorous or inspirational sayings, but they certainly are not the frilly, colorful, starched and ironed variety women once wore as a statement of pride in their roles as homemakers. They put their talents, energy, creativity, and ingenuity into serving their families, and they weren't afraid to say so.

Women still serve their families, some in the home and others in the workplace. They still honor their husbands and look after their children. They still take pride in doing the very best they can. Women have not changed, but the concept of service has. Somehow it has taken on a derogatory sense that steals the joy and satisfaction a woman feels in her role, however that role is now defined.

There is no shame in service to others. Jesus came as a servant to give Himself for humankind. When we follow His example by giving ourselves for others, He is pleased. Husbands and wives alike have been called by God to do just that by putting the needs of their families above their own.

Frilly, starched aprons may not be your style, but they were just a practical symbol anyway. Take pride and joy in serving your husband and children.

To My Husband

*I*n my eyes there lies no vision
But the sight of your dear face.
In my heart there is no feeling
But the warmth of your embrace.
In my mind there are no thoughts
But the thoughts of you, my dear.
In my soul no other longing
But just to have you near.
All my dreams were built around you
And I've come to know it's true,
In my life there is no living
That is not a part of you.

~HSR

New Blessings

Two people are better than one, because they get more done by working together. If one falls down, the other can help him up.
<small>ECCLESIASTES 4:9–10 NCV</small>

God commented on each part of His creation, saying that each part was good. But that was only until He made man. Then His comment was that it was not good for man to be alone, so He made Eve—a help-mate, a friend. Aren't you glad? How sad it would be if we had to live without other people.

In marriage you are part of a unit, and all the experiences that you survive—the good and the bad—bond you together by building your faith in each other. As you share your needs and emotions, there is someone who cares, understands, and loves you as you are.

Your dreams might be different; still you serve as companions to support one another in those dreams—by walking side by side, encouraging and comforting each other. Your triumphs will be sweeter because you have someone to rejoice with you. Your burdens will be lighter when the two of you are lifting them together.

Cling to your husband—depend on him. Even with his human faults, he can love, comfort, and point you to God. Become the same help to him. Time cannot diminish true love that is built on God's goodness and trustworthiness. You will only grow closer as the Lord planned all along when you become friends for life.

Celebrating
Our Family

IT'S SO NICE TO HAVE A DAD AROUND THE HOUSE

Dads are special people no home should be without,
For every family will agree they're so nice to have about.
They are a happy mixture of a small boy and a man,
And they're very necessary in every family plan.
Sometimes they're most demanding
and stern and firm and tough,
But underneath they're soft as silk, for this is just a bluff.
But in any kind of trouble Dad reaches out his hand,
And you can always count on him to
help and understand.
And while we do not praise Dad as often as we should,
We love him and admire him, and while
that's understood,
It's only fair to emphasize his importance and his worth,
For if there were no loving dads, this would
be a loveless earth.

~HSR

A FATHER AT HOME

"I will be a Father to you, and you will be my
sons and daughters, says the Lord Almighty."
2 CORINTHIANS 6:18

All children long for a father's love and attentive care. They want
and need someone to shelter them through the ups and downs of
life, someone who will teach them how to live. Of course, some have
wonderful fathers who give their children everything they need. Others
are not so fortunate.

Perhaps you had a missing father or one who did not live up to his
responsibilities. You might have even been a victim of neglect or abuse
at your father's hand. God wants you to know that He is there for you
regardless of the kind of earthly father you may have had. If your father
was a good man, loving and caring, you have probably realized your
heavenly Father is much the same only more. If your father was not
around or did not measure up, He is eager to be there in his place.

Our Father God is strong and steady, loving and caring, kind and
generous. He is everything a father should be and more. He has given
you His letter, the Bible, to help you understand more about life and
make good choices. Even the best earthly fathers fail us at one time or
another. They are subject to their humanity. But God's advice is flawless;
His love is uncompromised. Reach out and take His hand and you will
never again be without a father in your home.

31

My Father's Day Prayer

I said a Father's Day prayer for you—
I asked the Lord above
To keep you safely in His care
And enfold you in His love.
I did not ask for fortune,
For riches or for fame,
I only asked for blessings
In the Holy Savior's name—
Blessings to surround you
In times of trial and stress,
And inner joy to fill your heart
With peace and happiness.

~HSR

A Father's Love

He is a father to orphans, and he defends the widows.
God gives the lonely a home. He leads prisoners out with joy,
but those who turn against God will live in a dry land.
PSALM 68:5–6 NCV

Dad's gone and there is an empty chair at the table this week. Until he returns the house will seem strangely empty for a little girl who misses her dad so much. When this dedicated, loving man is away, his daughter struggles. She calls her dad often and prays for him.

Children need a father at home to guide them, encourage them, and show them they are loved. He represents a safe place in a frightening world, a source of strength and security.

As a father, you have a great responsibility not only to provide for your family's physical needs but also to be present in their lives, to offer guidance and encouragement, and to teach them good values and a reverence for God.

God knows you aren't perfect. He sees that you are a human being. All He asks is that you reach out to Him for help, do your best, and refuse to let your failures define your relationships with your children. He forgives freely, and so will they when they see that you are becoming the father God created you to be.

Men often make the mistake of thinking that caring for children is a woman's job, but the Bible tells us that fathers are the backbone of their families. Your family needs your love, wisdom, and encouragement.

33

IT TAKES A MOTHER

It takes a mother's love
   To make a house a home—
A place to be remembered
   No matter where we roam.
It takes a mother's patience
   To bring a child up right
And her courage and her cheerfulness
   To make a dark day bright.
It takes a mother's thoughtfulness
   To mend the heart's deep hurts
And her skill and her endurance
   To mend little socks and shirts.
It takes a mother's kindness
   To forgive us when we err,
To sympathize in trouble
   And to bow her head in prayer.
It takes a mother's wisdom
   To recognize our needs
And to give us reassurance
   By her loving words and deeds.

~HSR

CENTER OF THE HOME

Therefore comfort each other and edify one another,
just as you also are doing.
1 THESSALONIANS 5:11 NKJV

*M*others are considered to be the heart of their homes, and certainly as the mother, you try to bring a positive outlook and a can-do attitude to the family. You are there to love and support your husband and love and train your children as they learn to face the realities of life.

It's a big job! No doubt about it. It's difficult to keep up sometimes, and it's painful to see your children suffer with their own poor choices or insist on learning things the hard way. A wise woman remembers that God is her constant help. When you are tired and discouraged, bogged down in household chores, school and church schedules, and work deadlines, remember that God is fully committed to helping you make your house a home. When you stand as the center, the heart, the nucleus of your family, you are really representing Him. He works through you to bring stability and security to each day.

Set an example for your children by seeking God's help when you are unsure of the way. Teach your children to pray and to thank God for His wisdom, comfort, and encouragement through the hard places. These are things that will go with your children throughout their lives.

Sometimes being a good mother is the result of being a good daughter to your heavenly Father.

MOTHER IS A WORD
CALLED LOVE

Mother is a word called love,
  And all the world is mindful of
The love that's given and shown to others
  Is different from the love of mothers.
For mothers play the leading roles
  In giving birth to little souls—
For though small souls are heaven-sent
  We realize they're only lent. . .
No other love than mother love
  Could do the things required of
The one to whom God gives the keeping
  Of His wee lambs, awake or sleeping.
So mothers are a special race
  God sent to earth to take His place,
And "Mother" is a lovely name
  That even saints are proud to claim.

~HSR

A Mother's Heart

We were gentle among you, just as a nursing mother cherishes her own children.
1 Thessalonians 2:7 nkjv

The hen tenderly cares for her chicks even before they are hatched from the eggs. Then she herds them around the farmyard, teaching them what to eat and drink. She carefully guards them from predators. And at the sound of thunder, she gathers them up and shelters them under her wings. Not every human mother tends her children so well, and there is a reason.

God created animals to behave instinctively, but human beings have been given a free will. As a human mother, you have choices to make concerning how you will care for your children. So we see a vast range of parenting methods and results. How can you be assured that you are mothering your children properly?

The Bible provides advice and instruction. It also says that older Christian women should teach the younger ones how to look after their homes and love their husbands and children. A mentor in the form of a woman you trust and can talk to might be the best help you can find. Don't be afraid to seek help and inspiration from other moms.

As a mother you will make some mistakes, but God is your helper, and He cares for your children even more than you can with your human limitations. Put your faith in Him, and He will teach you how to be the caring mother your children need.

MOTHERS ARE SPECIAL PEOPLE

Mothers are special people
  In a million different ways,
And merit loving compliments
  And many words of praise.
For a mother's aspiration
  Is for her family's success,
To make the family proud of her
  And bring them happiness.
And like our heavenly Father,
  She's a patient, loving guide,
Someone we can count on
  To be always on our side.

~HSR

THE POWER OF WORDS

Careless words stab like a sword, but wise words bring healing.
PROVERBS 12:18 NCV

*P*icture a child who is told since birth that he is cherished and loved. Now imagine what damage would be done to a child's self-esteem if he were called "stupid" or "ugly" by his mother. Our words have the power to heal or harm. Damage done by words can be deep. The old schoolyard rhyme "Sticks and stones can break my bones, but words can never hurt me," is so untrue. Words can do immeasurable damage, especially words from the lips of a mother.

Of course, raising children is a difficult job, a stressful job. Some days you may be pushed to your breaking point. At those times, God can help you speak with words of encouragement, comfort, positive reinforcement, and patience. He can imbue you with the power to overcome anger, resentment, and frustration. If you suffered abuse as a child, God can heal those wounds and prevent the cycle of abuse from damaging another generation.

The words you long to hear—words of love, words of strength, words of wisdom—can guide them through the obstacle course that is life. Bless your child with words that instill hope and capture the essence of faith and goodness. Allow God to bring you to a stage of maturity that will show by the wise words you speak.

A MOTHER'S DAY PRAYER

*O*ur Father in heaven,
   Whose love is divine,
Thanks for the love
   Of a mother like mine.
In Thy great mercy
   Look down from above
And grant this dear mother
   The gift of Your love.

~HSR

WHO WALKS
BESIDE HER?

Whenever we have the opportunity, we should do good to everyone—
especially to those in the family of faith.
GALATIANS 6:10 NLT

A mother with several small children in tow and an infant
nestled in a snuggly sling struggles to get the little ones safely
from her car to the grocery store. She plunks one into the
shopping cart and trails the rest carefully behind her. People
seem not to notice that the woman could use a hand. Things
have changed from times when strangers would have offered
assistance and approved of the mother's courage and diligence.

Everyone knows that mothering is not an easy job. The
hours are long and the days devoid of adult conversation and
interaction. A mother can become lonely and discouraged,
yet God is aware of her hardship. Perhaps He has whispered
in your ear, urging you to step up beside a young mom and
offer a helping hand, a voice of advice, and a listening ear.

A mother who is devoted to her children deserves
support and respect. As a woman learns to die to her selfish
ways and give all for her children, you can be an encourager,
help her grow as a person and find fulfillment and
confidence in the difficult, but rich, work of motherhood.
Watching children grow and develop, both physically and
spiritually, is an awesome journey. Walk beside a mother on
her journey, and you, too, will be blessed.

A MOTHER'S LOVE

A mother's love is something
That no one can explain—
It is made of deep devotion
And of sacrifice and pain.
It is endless and unselfish and enduring,
Come what may,
For nothing can destroy it
Or take that love away.

~HSR

HIS ANGEL MOTHER

Her children stand and bless her. Her husband praises her.
PROVERBS 31:28 NLT

Her son stood up and called her blessed, and his words about her are still resounding. Abe Lincoln said, "All that I am or ever hope to be, I owe to my angel mother." Don't you hope that your children will praise you, too?

If you could see yourself from your children's perspective, what would you look like? Would social charms fool them? Would they see your love and concern for others? Would they see you as physically beautiful yet spiritually weak and faded? Would they see patience, generosity, and courage when they looked at you?

What did Lincoln's mother do that gave him the strength of character to lead a nation through a civil war? What was her home like? What mothering skills did she employ to raise a humble, honest, and obviously grateful son? Was it her situation, her fortune, or her example that made her precious in her son's eyes? Was it her wisdom?

All mothers long for such accolades. We want to be considered charming and beautiful. We want to be valued, praised, and honored. The woman who is honored will be that mother who seeks wisdom as Solomon did when God allowed him to ask for what he most desired. She will be that mother who pleases God by her faith and whose faith and love are obvious to all. What do your children see in you?

MOTHERHOOD

The dearest gifts that heaven holds,
    The very finest, too,
Were made into one pattern
    That was perfect, sweet, and true.
The angels smiled, well pleased, and said,
    "Compared to all the others,
This pattern is so wonderful
    Let's use it just for mothers!"
And through the years, a mother has been
    All that's sweet and good,
For there's a bit of God and love
    In all true motherhood.

~HSR

GOD'S REACHING LOVE

"How often I've longed to gather your children, gather your children like a hen, her brood safe under her wings—but you refused and turned away!"
LUKE 13:34 MSG

*H*ave you ever been pushed away by a small child who is struggling to do something he isn't yet capable of doing? Have you had to stand back and allow a child the freedom to struggle and fail? As a mother you have the opportunity to love your children like God loves His. What a task! What a challenge! How fearful and wonderful!

God reaches out to His children with love—stretching, drawing, hoping His advice will help them escape danger. He endeavors to give them the wisdom they need to live long, satisfying lives. He wants to see them prosper and make the most of the talents and abilities He has placed within them. Isn't that what you want for your children?

God also knows that His children do not always make good choices with the freedom and independence He has given them. He knows how a mother feels when her children pull away. He knows the pain of pushing a fledgling from the nest and watching to see if that young bird will falter or fly. And He knows the joy of seeing one soar.

God knows how to be a good mother, and He has placed those same instincts in you. With His help you will become the mother He created you to be.

The Greatest Career Is Womanhood

So glad a tiny baby came
    To share your life and love and name,
For no doubt she is the greatest claim
    That you have ever had to fame.
And don't misunderstand me, dear,
    You were a star in your career,
But what, I ask you, is success
    Compared with heaven's happiness?
And how could plaudits anywhere
    Be half as wonderful and fair?
For this experience of the heart
    Surpasses any skill or art,
For man excels in every line
    But woman has a gift divine,
And in this world there is no other
    As greatly honored as a mother.

~HSR

FITTING INTO GOD'S PLAN

Each of you should look not only to your own interests,
but also to the interests of others.
PHILIPPIANS 2:4

*T*aking part in the plan of God for your life is the path to finding
happiness. If God blesses you with children, you will find joy and
fulfillment in the mothering of those little people. Shepherding the
hearts of children, providing for their physical and emotional needs,
and preparing them to be successful adults is a great calling and one
that can bring you happiness and satisfaction.

You may also be a doctor, a lawyer, a writer, a chef, or an office
manager. You may be a teacher, or a businesswoman. There are few
limitations for women these days. You can become anything you
want to be. But if you have children, you must remember that being
a mother is your first career. Growing children have hearts that
need almost constant ministering to. They need the strong, stable
environment your presence provides for them.

Children change from infants to adults in just a few years. It is in
the home that children learn to live their lives successfully and love God
with all their hearts. They need all the wisdom and guidance you can
give them.

Caring for a home and children can be overwhelming. Ask God
to help you become the encourager, the helper, the mentor, the teacher
your children need as they prepare for life.

What Is a Baby?

A baby is a gift of life
    Born of the wonder of love—
A little bit of eternity
    Sent from the Father above,
Giving a new dimension
    To the love between husband and wife
And putting an added new meaning
    To the wonder and mystery of life.

~HSR

ARROWS IN A QUIVER

Like arrows in the hand of a warrior are sons born in one's youth.
Blessed is the man whose quiver is full of them.
PSALM 127:4–5

The students lined up and shot their arrows on cue of the archery coach's whistle. Two stuck in the bull's-eyes; all others, but one, struck within the colored circles. That stray arrow whizzed past the target and hit a backdrop. It fell to the ground yards from its goal.

Psalm 127 compares children to arrows and parents to archers. Can you picture arrows shooting fast and straight from the bow? If the archer is trained and skilled, he takes aim, allowing nothing to distract his eye. He pulls back the bowstring and stands straight and strong so that his arrow will fly smooth and fast to hit its mark.

What skills do you need as a parent? As a new mom you may have begun like those archery students with little or no training for the task of parenting. You need God's helping hand, like that of the archery coach, showing you the proper stance to take, how to grip the bow, how to send your children like arrows on their journey into the world. Only with God's expert help can you gain the skill to be a great parent.

You want to be able to release your son or daughter at just the best time, when he or she is stable and ready and the target is in sight. You will be watching, hoping, and praying that your child will do well in life and stay true and honorable. So shoulders back, arm straight, take careful aim!

BABY

A wee bit of heaven
　　Drifted down from above—
A handful of happiness,
　　A heart full of love.
The mystery of life
　　So sacred and sweet,
The giver of joy
　　So deep and complete.
Precious and priceless,
　　So lovable, too—
The world's sweetest miracle,
　　Baby, is you.

~HSR

Treasured Child

I, too, was once my father's son, tenderly loved as my mother's only child.
PROVERBS 4:3 NLT

Nothing is sweeter than a newborn baby. The oohs and aahs over a little bundle of joy are sure to follow a new mama everywhere she takes her baby. People just can't resist a miniature person so seemingly innocent and perfect.

That baby, though completely dependent on his or her parents, is full of potential. In only a few years, he or she may be leading Congress or heading a corporation. He may be building a home, driving a truck, or calculating taxes. She may be setting supper on the table for a family of her own, teaching school, clerking in a grocery store, or singing on a stage. That cute, tiny bundle has limitless potential.

Mother and father help the baby grow physically and spiritually, emotionally and intellectually, so that she will be ready and able to reach beyond herself and follow her dreams. They teach and mentor him to become the person God created him to be.

As the baby changes from an infant into a child, then a teen, then a young adult, his parents will cherish him and hold tightly to their hopes for him. Will the child falter? Almost certainly to some degree. He or she will need encouragement, understanding, and forgiveness, which loving parents are happy to give.

Every child has potential. Can you see it? Reach out to help a child in your life navigate the path to maturity.

MOTHERS WERE
ONCE DAUGHTERS

Every home should have a daughter,
   For there's nothing like a girl
To keep the world around her
   In one continuous whirl. . . .
And someday in the future,
   If it be God's gracious will,
She, too, will be a mother
   And know that reverent thrill
That comes to every mother
   Whose heart is filled with love
When she beholds the angel
   That God sent her from above.
And there would be no life at all
   In this world or the other
Without a darling daughter
   Who in turn becomes a mother.

~HSR

TRUE BEAUTY

Charm can fool you, and beauty can trick you,
but a woman who respects the Lord should be praised.
PROVERBS 31:30 NCV

A middle-aged woman spent some time in the greeting card aisle looking for just the right birthday card. She was looking for one with the word *beautiful*, because that's exactly how she would describe her daughter. She searched for a card that spoke of the joy and hope that beautiful daughter had brought to her life, one that expressed how deeply she would always be loved and cherished.

All mothers think their daughters are beautiful; but some, the woman in the greeting card aisle included, know that their daughters possess more than natural good looks. These young women glow with inner peace. They behave with grace and wisdom because they reverence God. They walk with confidence because their self-esteem is rooted in God.

If you are the mother of such a daughter, you are blessed indeed. Encourage her to continue to walk as a woman of God, and continue to set an example for her. Let her see your good works and pure heart. Ask her to join you in performing acts of kindness and charity. Teach her to fight to become all God created her to be. Show her how to be truly beautiful.

The lessons you teach her today may one day be the lessons she teaches her own daughter, creating a chain of true and lasting beauty.

To My Sister

If I knew the place where wishes come true,
    That's where I would go for my wish for you,
And I'd wish you all that you're wishing for,
    For no sister on earth deserves it more.
But trials and troubles come to us all,
    For that's the way we grow heaven-tall.
And my birthday prayer to our Father above
    Is to keep you safe in His infinite love,
And we both know that gifts don't mean much
    Compared to our love and God's blessed touch.

~HSR

WISDOM, MY SISTER

Treat wisdom as a sister, and make
understanding your closest friend.
PROVERBS 7:4 NCV

A sister knows how to encourage you when you are
down. A sister loves you with a special love. She can
give advice and teach you much about the challenges of
life, yet she is able to call out the best characteristics in
you. What, then, would it be like to call Wisdom your
sister—to draw her so close that you could live with her
continual guidance?

Solomon, considered to be the wisest man ever to
live, called wisdom the principal thing a person should
seek to obtain. He advises you to embrace her, to hold
on to her, just as you would a trustworthy sibling.

Sisters are better than friends. They aren't afraid to
tell you the difficult truth and challenge you to move
forward in the face of hardship and trouble. In the same
way, wisdom won't coddle you. It will call you to action,
back you up, teach you to be honest and faithful, and
help you be your best in every situation.

If you grew up with a good sister, you are blessed.
You probably found her to be a trusted confidant,
protector, and advocate. Wisdom can be trusted as well.
It will inspire you and provide you with courage and
strength. Whatever circumstances you may face, treat
wisdom like a sister!

SHE'S LIVING STILL

Since mother went away,
It seems she's nearer than before,
I cannot touch her hand,
And yet she's with me more and more,
And the years have never lessened
The longing in my heart
That came the day I realized
That we must dwell apart,
And just as long as memory lives,
My mother cannot die,
For in my heart she's living still
As passing years go by.

~HSR

FORK AND SPOON

*We want you to know what will happen to the believers who have
died so you will not grieve like people who have no hope.*
1 THESSALONIANS 4:13 NLT

*S*he was buried with a fork and spoon in her hand. The preacher said
she had asked him to tell everyone she was headed for God's feasting
table in heaven. This would be a meal she didn't have to cook! You can't
be sad with a funeral message like that, especially for a woman who
spent her life serving her family.

If you have lost a mother and hurt for her absence, it is comforting
to know that her teachings, words, and deeds can live on in your mind
and heart—that you can carry her memory there and have a part of her
with you.

The Bible assures us that we don't have to grieve like people who
don't have any hope when someone we love dies. Our faith in God
assures us that we will someday be reunited with parents, children,
family, and friends who go before us into heaven. With that hope
we can go on with our daily lives and need not despair when we lose
someone.

Think about your mother and the life she lived. Imagine her as
she was with the utensils of her work in her hands. Envision her at the
feasting table with an empty chair for you waiting beside hers. Comfort
yourself in knowing that a day will come when we will be joyfully
together in heaven with our Lord.

Celebrating Love, Joy, and Gladness

THE MAGIC OF LOVE

Love is like magic and it always will be,
   For love still remains life's sweet mystery.
Love works in ways that are wondrous and strange,
   And there's nothing in life that love cannot change.
Love can transform the most commonplace
   Into beauty and splendor and sweetness and grace.
Love is unselfish, understanding, and kind,
   For it sees with its heart and not with its mind.
Love gives and forgives; there is nothing too much
   For love to heal with its magic touch.
Love is the language that every heart speaks,
   For love is the one thing that every heart seeks.
And where there is love, God, too, will abide
   And bless the family residing inside.

~HSR

LOVING OTHERS

Live a life filled with love, following the example of Christ.
He loved us and offered himself as a sacrifice for us, a pleasing aroma to God.
EPHESIANS 5:2 NLT

A natural disaster such as the hurricane that hit New Orleans a few years ago demonstrates the compassion and desire to help others that God has placed within each of us. You've doubtless seen it at the scene of a house fire or the search for a missing child. Some volunteers give money, some build homes, and others give their blood to help those in need.

It is in this way that we see how we are created in God's image, for He is full of compassion and lovingkindness. Jesus set the ultimate example by giving up His place in heaven and coming to earth to rescue us from the penalty of our disobedience. While He was here, He did more than redeem us; He also ministered to the many and various needs of the people He encountered. He reached out to the poor, orphans, widows, the sick, and the disabled. Jesus loved even those who didn't recognize Him, and He fought for everyone, even those who could not return the favor.

What can you do today to show your love for God and your concern for others? How can you live a life of love, like Christ did? You must know someone who could use some encouragement or a helping hand. Reach out with all the compassion and kindness God has placed within you.

Be Glad

Be glad that your life has
been full and complete,
Be glad that you've tasted
the bitter and sweet.
Be glad that you've walked
in sunshine and rain,
Be glad that you've felt
both pleasure and pain.
Be glad that you've had
such a full, happy life,
Be glad for your joy as well as your strife.
Be glad that you've walked
with courage each day,
Be glad you've had strength
for each step of the way.
Be glad for the comfort that
you've found in prayer.
Be glad for God's blessings,
His love, and His care.

~HSR

A Thankful Heart

Be joyful always; pray continually; give thanks in all circumstances,
for this is God's will for you in Christ Jesus.
1 Thessalonians 5:16–18

*S*he tried her best to stay cheerful. Even when hardships
came her way, she hoped to be able to pull off a smile and a
song like Paul and Silas did when they were wrongfully locked
in a jail cell. *How did those two men find the strength to sing
when they were so badly treated?* she wondered.

They surely weren't happy or even cheerful in their hard
circumstances, yet they were joyful. Cheer is momentary and
can disappear in a flash. Happiness is only a transient thing,
but joy is a condition of the heart, the result of being loved
and forgiven and in right relationship with God.

You can face trouble with joy in your heart, knowing your
heavenly Father is with you. Being thankful for the good and
also for what you may define as the bad will allow you to see
the blessing in even the most painful situations.

God wants you to experience joy rather than a fleeting
moment of happiness. He wants you to revel in the knowledge
that you are never alone. He is with you, helping you to find
the rainbow in the rain, the sweet honey in the sting of the
bee, and the rose among the thorns. Cheerfulness is a precious
blessing, but joyfulness gives you the strength to sing even
from a jail cell.

A Sure Way to a Happy Day

Happiness is something we create in our minds;
    It's not something you search for and so seldom find.
It's just waking up and beginning the day
    By counting our blessings and kneeling to pray.
It's giving up thoughts that breed discontent
    And accepting what comes as a gift heaven-sent.
It's giving up wishing for things we have not
    And making the best of whatever we've got.
It's knowing that life is determined for us
    And pursuing our tasks without fret, fume, or fuss.
For it's by completing what God gives us to do
    That we find real contentment and happiness, too.

~HSR

FINDING ENOUGH

Elisha said to her, "What shall I do for you?
Tell me, what do you have in the house?" And she said,
"Your maidservant has nothing in the house but a jar of oil."
2 KINGS 4:2 NKJV

*S*ome women really do desire to reach out and touch the lives of others. They see the needs around them and feel the urge to step up and help. Unfortunately, with every idea comes a reason why they aren't able to follow through.

Some may feel they don't have the time and energy necessary after caring for the needs of their own families. Others may believe their homes aren't big enough to host a Bible study or nice enough to invite a lonely neighbor to lunch. Somehow they don't feel they have what it takes to do what God is asking.

Is this the way you feel? Are you concerned that you lack the skills, the talent, the wardrobe, or the stamina to follow through with those things God whispers in your ear? Elisha asked the widow, "What do you have?" She had only a little bottle of oil, but that was all she needed to save her home and children.

When God prompts you to do some act of kindness or calls you to reach out to someone, step out by faith and trust Him to provide. You will soon learn that He never asks you to do anything you are powerless to accomplish. He will take what you have and make it enough.

THE GIFT OF LASTING LOVE

*L*ove is much more than a tender caress
    And more than bright hours of happiness,
For a lasting love is made up of sharing
    Both hours that are joyous and also despairing.
It's made up of patience and deep understanding
    And never of stubborn or selfish demanding
It's made up of climbing the steep hills together
    And facing with courage life's stormiest weather.
And nothing on earth or in heaven can part
    A love that has grown to be part of the heart
And just like the sun and the stars and the sea,
    This love will go on through eternity,
For true love lives on when earthly things die,
    For it's part of the spirit that soars to the sky.

~HSR

Amazing Love

Though one may be overpowered, two can defend themselves.
A cord of three strands is not quickly broken.
Ecclesiastes 4:12

Returning from her honeymoon, a woman was injured so severely in a car accident that she did not remember the wedding or ever meeting her new spouse. What did the young man do when his new wife claimed she never had known him? Despite his hurt, he stayed with his wife and cared for her while she recovered.

Most newlyweds think their love for each other is the strongest bond on earth, yet when trouble comes and impossible odds stack up against them, will it be strong enough to pull them through? It can be, because when it is strengthened by God's love, it is like a rope with three strands twisted tightly together.

God loved you before you cared about Him and before you knew Him. He kept loving you no matter what happened. With His help, you and your spouse can build an enduring love that survives hardships—even those as daunting as the one faced by this remarkable young husband.

God's love for you is not based on your inherent goodness. Rather, it is based on His decision to love you at the expense of His life. It is difficult to perceive the power of God's love for us, but basing your marriage on such love translates into a tie strong enough for a lifetime.

Warm Our Hearts
with Thy Love

*O*h, God, who made the summer
    And warmed the earth with beauty,
Warm our hearts with gratitude
    And devotion to our duty. . . .
Oh God, look down on our cold hearts
    And warm them with Your love,
And grant us Your forgiveness
    Which we're so unworthy of.

~HSR

GIVE COMPASSION
A VOICE

Everyone enjoys a fitting reply; it is wonderful
to say the right thing at the right time!
PROVERBS 15:23 NLT

The young father felt he had tried everything and that he couldn't go on until the words of a child touched his heart. The child had drawn a big heart on a white sheet of construction paper. The Valentine's message, written in bright red letters, read: "Jesus loves you and I do, too!" Has one simple phrase of encouragement come to you at a needy moment?

Words of comfort can deliver more healing to a grief-stricken heart than hours of fancy preaching. The Bible says good words enhance life. Wholesome words are like a tree that gives life. Kind words are sweet like honey. Just having a cheerful face can do more good for you and those you meet than medicine. Have you ever been down or afraid then an unexpected smile or a simple greeting made all the difference to your heart?

We have all spoken and been the recipient of words that stung and discouraged. God speaks words that are wise and pure and set a standard of kindness. Our words should speak up for the poor and the needy and those who can't defend themselves.

Your words could do more than you can imagine for those who hear them. If you speak well-ordered and well-seasoned words, you will be like a life-giving stream of pure water leaving a trail of courage and life behind.

WHAT IS LOVE?

What is love? No words can define it—
    It's something so great only God could design it.
Wonder of wonders, beyond man's conception—
    And only in God can love find true perfection. . . .
For love is unselfish, giving more than it takes—
    And no matter what happens, love never forsakes.
It's faithful and trusting and always believing,
    Guileless and honest and never deceiving.
Yes, love is beyond what man can define,
    For love is immortal and God's gift is divine!

~HSR

UNDER THE COLD SNOW

Christ's love is greater than anyone can ever know,
but I pray that you will be able to know that love.
Then you can be filled with the fullness of God.
EPHESIANS 3:19 NCV

Day dawned and the children ran to the windows. The entire world seemed to have disappeared under a white blanket of snow. Dry winter grass and bare shrubbery, the garden rows, bicycles, yard toys, the mailbox, the doghouse, even the driveway were covered. Not a breath stirred. Everything seemed frozen in time.

No lights came on. Breakfast was a cold one. The snowstorm had knocked out the power. School was dismissed, but no cartoons would entertain. An oil lamp and a few candles were brought out to add light to the cold, dark rooms. The storm seemed to overwhelm—to stop everything and everyone.

But under the snow, life was stirring in the roots of the grasses and trees. Small animals began to scurry and hunt for a meal. Birds began to show up for handouts. The snow dribbled and dripped and softened because there was life and heat below the surface. The snow only covered for a while; then it melted away and soaked into the ground and evaporated into the sky.

Your troubles can feel like that sometimes, covering you like a blanket until you can barely breathe. But if love is strong, it melts the cold of hurt and tribulation. It warms your heart and keeps you alive. What has love seen you through?

Celebrating Our Blessings and Memories

Showers of Blessings

Each day there are showers of blessings
Sent from the Father above,
For God is a great, lavish giver,
And there is no end to His love.
And His grace is more than sufficient,
His mercy is boundless and deep,
And His infinite blessings are countless—
And all this we're given to keep
If we but seek God and find Him
And ask for a bounteous measure
Of this wholly immeasurable offering
From God's inexhaustible treasure.
For no matter how big man's dreams are,
God's blessings are infinitely more,
For always God's giving is greater
Than what man is asking for.

~HSR

Rain On!

*When he thunders, the waters in the heavens roar;
he makes clouds rise from the ends of the earth. He sends lightning
with the rain and brings out the wind from his storehouses.*

JEREMIAH 10:13

The rain was a "gully washer," racing along the ditches and off to fill some lake or pond. The thunder rumbled and boomed, and lightning streaked across the dark skies. What do you think about during a heavy rain? Do you wonder if it would be possible to count all the raindrops? How many does it take to quench the thirst of an oak tree, to fill a pond, to refresh the earth?

It would be easier to count the raindrops than to count the blessings God pours out on you every day. Blessings around you go almost unnoticed—the air you breathe, the clouds overhead, the whoosh of the wind in the treetops, the rain itself. An old hymn says that if the sky were a huge scroll of paper and the ocean filled with ink, it would not be enough to write about all the love God has for us.

Rain—people love the sound of it on the rooftops. We pray for rain to fall on our fields and forests. Next time it rains, watch the drops fall and think of a blessing for each drop. You won't be able to do it, will you? There are so many—so many you cannot fully realize the number—a plethora of blessings every single day. Thank the Lord and let it rain on!

HEART GIFTS

*I*t's not the things that can be bought
    That are life's richest treasures,
It's just the little gifts from the heart
    That money cannot measure.
A cheerful smile, a friendly word,
    A sympathetic nod,
All priceless little treasures
    From the storehouse of our God.
They are the things that can't be bought
    With silver or with gold,
For thoughtfulness and kindness
    And love are never sold.
They are the priceless things in life
    For which no one can pay,
And the giver finds rich recompense
    In giving them away.

~HSR

SHOW LOVE AT HOME

"Then the King will say, 'I'm telling the solemn truth:
Whenever you did one of these things to someone overlooked or ignored,
that was me—you did it to me.'"
MATTHEW 25:40 MSG

A young mother fell and broke her wrist. The cast, which covered her right hand and arm all the way to her elbow, was difficult to manage, especially for the mother of a toddler. She could do it, but it certainly wasn't easy. Between shifts, a friend came to visit. Looking for some way to help, she noticed the young mother's nails. She soaked and gently washed the injured hand and trimmed and filed the fingernails. Then she massaged lotion into the dry skin. It was a gift of kindness not easily forgotten.

Have you ever been in a difficult situation and someone took the time to reach out to you in kindness? Being the recipient of such an act shows how much the small things we do for others matter. How loud an act of mercy can speak!

Perhaps you are the type to do sweet things for friends and coworkers. How about family? Have you looked around lately and noted a family member who could use some attention and caring? If you find a way to fill the need, the kindness may engender more good works. You could start something great.

One small act can build trust and appreciation at home where you need it most. Can you imagine the love and the joy that a habit of selfless acts could bring to your house?

Put Your Problems in God's Hands for He Completely Understands

Although it sometimes seems to us
  Our prayers have not been heard,
God always knows our every need
  Without a single word.
And He will not forsake us
  Even though the way is steep,
For always He is near to us,
  A tender watch to keep.
And in good time He will answer us,
  And in His love He'll send
Greater things than we have asked
  And blessings without end.
So though we do not understand
  Why trouble comes to man,
Can we not be contented
  Just to know it is God's plan?

~HSR

WAITING ON GOD

You can be sure that God will take care of everything you need,
his generosity exceeding even yours in the glory that pours from Jesus.
PHILIPPIANS 4:19 MSG

Standing in line, sitting in traffic, pacing in front of the microwave, waiting for your computer to boot up or the doctor to call. Perhaps you enjoy the pause such situations create, but most people see them as a waste of time and a source of irritation.

Not all waiting is a waste of time, however. When you are waiting and watching for an answer to prayer, God is giving you a chance to wait on Him, to be seated for a few minutes in His throne room. He may feel you need time to think about what you have asked for and how it will impact your life. He may be giving you an opportunity to see another point of view or correct an error in your own thought process. Or God may feel that a "pregnant" pause is a good way to impress on you the true value of the answer He is sending your way.

Waiting on God is one of the most blessed places you can be as His child. During that time, you are focused on His presence and His priorities, poised to listen for His voice. If you find yourself in a place of waiting on God, see the experience as a gift in itself and cherish every moment.

MEMORY RENDEZVOUS

Memory builds a little pathway
    That goes winding through my heart.
It's a lovely, quiet, gentle trail
    From other things apart.
I only meet when traveling there
    The folks I like the best,
For this road I call remembrance
    Is hidden from the rest,
But I hope I'll always find you
    In my memory rendezvous,
For I keep this little secret place
    To meet with folks like you.

~HSR

FRIENDS TO CHERISH

A real friend will be more loyal than a brother.
PROVERBS 18:24 NCV

It's an amazing experience when you meet someone you feel you've known forever—someone you realized immediately would be a special addition to your life. There is a feeling of closeness, a camaraderie, in some friendships from the first moment of acquaintance. These are the precious friends, the ones you hope will always be in your life. Meeting this kind of friend seems to be a miracle, prearranged and destined to be.

Even if time or miles separate you, there is a link that keeps your hearts together. The link is a memory the two of you shared while you were together. It may be a simple thing like a favorite food, a particular place, the scent of a flower, or the melody of a song you both loved.

Life has a way of moving mercilessly on. Quickly the years come and go. You'll want to remember special times you spent together. Snapshots fade and mementos are lost, but recollections tucked into your heart will be yours to keep.

As you share time with your forever friend, record those memories in your heart to call back to mind someday. Friendships are precious, so cherish and nurture them. Remember to thank God for the friendships that last. After all, He is the best friend you'll ever have.

THE HAPPINESS YOU ALREADY HAVE

*M*emories are treasures
   That time cannot destroy;
They are the happy pathway
   To yesterday's bright joy.

~HSR

SHARING MEMORIES

Good people leave their wealth to their grandchildren.
PROVERBS 13:22 NCV

W ho is she?" asks the little brown-eyed girl nestling beside her grandmother on the sofa.

"Why, she was my aunt Annie. She was just a young woman then in high school. After she graduated, she worked at the five-and-dime store for a year or two, and then she married Uncle Gerald."

The pages of the album turn, and the two laugh, point, and talk about graduations, weddings, babies in frilly dresses, toddlers, houses, vacations, relatives, and Christmas trees. If you ever spent an afternoon perusing a family photo album or clicking through a computer slideshow with your children or grandchildren, you remembered days gone by and made a new memory in the process.

The gift of family memories, a wealth of stories, and a billion little recollections are a treasure trove that God has blessed us with. Recalling the days of our lives helps us assess the passage of time so that we can appreciate that it is passing swiftly and resolve to live each day to its fullest.

We cherish our memories. They identify us—show us who we are and how we have lived. They stabilize us in our fast-moving world. They give us a sense of belonging, a grip on the past, and a hope for the future. Share your memories with another generation, and as you turn the pages, allow God to establish you and give you peace.

Celebrating with Thankful Hearts

Things to Be Thankful For

The good, green earth beneath our feet,
　　The air we breathe, the food we eat,
Some work to do, a goal to win,
　　A hidden longing deep within
That spurs us on to bigger things
　　And helps us meet what each day brings—
All these things and many more
　　Are things we should be thankful for. . . .
And most of all, our thankful prayers
　　Should rise to God because He cares.

~HSR

Name Them
One by One

*The blessing of the Lord brings wealth,
and he adds no trouble to it.*
PROVERBS 10:22

She had definitely begun that most precarious of all declines in life: She had begun to feel sorry for herself. Her friends seemed to be carefree. They seemed to be more attractive, smarter, and more organized; they were excellent cooks; and they had lovely, well-behaved children and beautiful wardrobes. They seemed to have happier marriages and sweeter relatives and nicer furnishings in better homes.

She reached with a heavy sigh to gather the supper dishes from the table, when the paper caught her eye. A scruffy, rather laboriously scribbled sentence stopped her and brought tears to her eyes. "You are my favorite mom in the whole world," her young son had scrawled.

A moment like this can break the blinders off our eyes and allow us to see all the true treasures and blessings God gives us that self-pity and frustration, envy and discontent cause us to forget. An old hymn admonished people to count their blessings—name them one by one. Not a bad plan, especially during tough times.

How has God blessed you? Sit down and renew your mind with the richness of God's mercy and grace, His amazing generosity. It's easy to spot in your children's smiles, your husband's loving eyes, your friends' words of encouragement. No matter what you may think you lack, focus on what God has given you.

So Many Reasons
to Love God

Thank You, God, for little things
    That come unexpectedly
To brighten up a dreary day
    That dawned so dismally.
Thank You, God, for sending
    A happy thought my way
To blot out my depression
    On a disappointing day.
Thank You, God, for brushing
    The dark clouds from my mind
And leaving only sunshine
    And joy of heart behind.

~HSR

The Great King

No nation on earth has ever been ruled by a king like the one we serve. Unlike other kings who demand service and allegiance, God rules by serving His citizens from the lowliest to the greatest. He cares so much for you that He not only will talk with you, guide you through trials, and help you make decisions, but He laid down His life for you. He loves us, each one of us, and He calls us His fellow workers, friends, and children.

God is fair and just in all His rulings. He is true to His word and keeps every promise. When has there ever been a ruler, a king, an elected official like Him? Never! He is completely honest and wholly infallible. He always chooses what is best for us and then allows us to make our own choices.

You may not realize that, though He is powerful, He wants you to stay close to Him so He can bless you and meet your needs.

God reigns with compassion and love, and though He has no parliament to oversee Him, He needs none. He is great in power yet, like a loving father, is concerned for you. Doesn't that make you want to love Him in return? You can count it a privilege to be a citizen of His eternal kingdom.

THANK YOU, GOD, FOR EVERYTHING

Thank You, God, for everything—
    The big things and the small
For every good gift comes from God,
    The giver of them all.
And all too often we accept
    Without any thanks or praise
The gifts God sends as blessings
    Each day in many ways.
And so at this time
    We offer up a prayer
To thank You, God, for giving us
    A lot more than our share.

~*HSR*

GOD'S TRUE COLORS

God looked at everything he had made, and it was very good.
Evening passed, and morning came. This was the sixth day.
GENESIS 1:31 NCV

*P*icture God holding a palette and a paintbrush. The palette is covered with generous mounds of paint—all the brightest and merriest colors of the universe.

There is the red of a tomato, the purple of a juicy plum, the soft shade of a peach wrapped in its crimson velvet fur, the fresh green of lettuce, the blue of blueberries, the brown speckles of a golden Asian pear, the sweet yellow of pineapple, and the curious purple-black of eggplant.

What if God had made all our fruits and vegetables the same color, size, shape, and texture? Isn't it enough that He feeds us? Isn't it grand of Him to give us such amazing diversity?

What if all the birds were the same, instead of the thousands of species? What if plants and flowers all looked alike? What if there were no bluebonnets, daisies, violets, or Indian paintbrushes, only red roses? What if trees were all covered with the same shade and color leaves, the same bark, and the same-sized branches? God took great care to design the world beautifully for you. He knew that because you were created in His image you would crave variety and beauty. The uniqueness of all God provided for you shows how much He cherishes you. Why else pomegranate? Why else kiwi?

A THANKFUL HEART

Take nothing for granted,
For whenever you do,
The joy of enjoying
Is lessened for you. . . .
For the joy of enjoying
And the fullness of living
Are found in the heart
That is filled with thanksgiving.

~HSR

Just a Word

*The right word spoken at the right time is
as beautiful as gold apples in a silver bowl.*
PROVERBS 25:11 NCV

A card in the mail, a pat on the back from your boss, a smile from
your spouse, or a "Great supper, Mom!" from your teenager warms your
heart and encourages you. Such small acts of gratitude have a positive
effect on a person. A word of gratitude changes our attitudes toward
work and people. Do you know how gratitude feels from the giving side?

Do you show gratitude for all God has done for you? The men
healed by Jesus were so thrilled by what they had received that they
rushed off without saying thank You, and that was so wrong. Jesus
commended only the one who returned to thank Him.

We should always notice the hand of God in our lives and see
to it that we tell Him how much we appreciate His goodness and
faithfulness to us. Such generosity from a fellow human being would
surely evoke thanks from us. Do we forget the Lord because we can't see
Him? Are we blinded to His wonders because of our busy schedules?

Spend some time each day noticing His gifts and thanking Him.
He does not change, and His attitude doesn't need improvement, but
giving thanks does the giver as much good as the receiver. You are sure
to be changed as you stop to say, "Thanks, God."

WHERE CAN WE FIND HIM?

*I*t's true we have never looked on His face,
But His likeness shines forth from
every place,
For the hand of God is everywhere
Along life's busy thoroughfare,
And His presence can be felt and seen
Right in the midst of our daily routine.
Things we touch and see and feel
Are what make God so very real.

~HSR

The Web of Life

The spider skillfully grasps with its hands, and it is in kings' palaces.
PROVERBS 30:28 NKJV

A trip out early on a misty morning seems otherworldly. Things feel and look different in the first light of dawn. The white circles of a spider's web in the dewy grass along the roadside look like patches of frost. Frost on such a morning is nonexistent, but every web shows up when it is heavy with dew and lit with the silvery light of early morning. How many webs fill the fence's spaces and run from signpost to tree branch! How many webs show up along the tall tufts of grass and stretch to the stems of wildflowers! The landscape looks covered with a jumble of lace pieces freshly washed and laid out to dry.

The webs are alike, and yet each one is different. Each is crafted by a tiny spider—woven of the silk filigree its body produces. Each work of art is a trap to catch breakfast from the air.

Even if you have never opened a Bible or heard the message of God's great love for you, He has written love messages to you everywhere you look. Even if you have not been aware of His majesty and power, seeing the world awaken in the early light and inspecting the impossibility of a silvery spider's web should be enough to tell you that God is real and wants to be part of your life.

FOREVER THANKS

Give thanks for the blessings
       That daily are ours—
The warmth of the sun,
       The fragrance of flowers.
With thanks for all the thoughtful,
       Caring things you always do
And a loving wish for happiness
       Today and all year through!

~HSR

A PRAYER FOR OUR FAMILY

Lord, I pray that You will be with us, that You will be seated with us at our table, stand beside us as we do our work, walk with us in the coolness of the evenings, and speak with us in the first light of the morning. Mend and blend our hearts until we are a strong unit that doesn't fear the present, the past, or the future. Go with us, Lord, and live with us.
Amen.